Those '70s Songs

44 Great Songs That Defined an Era

ISBN 1-57560-571-6

Visit our website at www.cherrylane.com

Contents

Afternoon Delight

Words and Music by
Bill Danoff

In a moderately slow country 2

Gon - na find my ba - by, gon - na hold her tight, gon - na grab some af - ter - noon ____ de - light. ____ My mot - to's al - ways been "When it's right, it's right," why wait un - til the mid - dle of a cold, dark night

When ev-'ry-thing's a lit-tle clear-er in the light of day, _____

And _____ we know the night is al-ways gon-na be here an-y-way? _____

(1.,3.) Think-ing of you's work-ing up my
(2.) out ___ this ___ morn-ing feel-ing

ap-pe-tite, look-ing for-ward to a lit-tle af-ter-noon de-light. _ Rub-bing
so po-lite, I al-ways thought a fish could not be caught who did-n't bite. _ But you

sticks and stones to-geth-er make the sparks ig-nite And the thought of rub-bing you is get-ting
got some bait a-wait-ing and I think I might Like_ nib-bl-ing a lit-tle af-ter-

so ex - cit - ing. Sky rock - ets in flight,
noon de - light. ___

Af - ter - noon _ de - light,

af - ter - noon _ de - light,

American Woman

Written by
Burton Cummings, Randy Bachman,
Gary Peterson and Jim Kale

9

A - mer - i - can Wom - an,____ gon - na mess your mind.____ I say, A,____

I say M,____ I say E,____ I say R,____ say I,____

use C,____ say A,____ N.____

A - mer - i - can Wom - an,____ gon - na mess your mind.____

A - mer - i - can Wom - an,____ gon - na mess your mind.____

A - mer-i-can Wom-an,___ gon-na mess your mind.___

ritard.

Somewhat slower (a tempo)

Chorus:

A - mer - i - can Wom-

- an,___ stay a - way from me,___ A - mer - i - can Wom-

- an,___ ma - ma let me be.___

Don't come hang-in' a - round_ my door,___ I don't wan-na see your face_ no more,

I got more im-por-tant things to do__ than spend my time__ grow-in' old with you.__ Now

wom-an,__ I said stay a - way,__ A - mer-i - can Wom-

- an,__ lis - ten what I say.

A - mer-i - can Wom-

- an,__ ma - ma let me be.__

E

Go, got-ta get a-way, got-ta get a-way, now go go go,— I'm gon-na

leave you, wom-an,— gon-na leave you wom-an.— Bye

bye,— Bye bye,— Bye bye,— Bye bye.— 1. You're

Fade E

ad lib.
melody

1. no good for me,   I'm no good for you.
2. Gonna look you right in the eye,   tell you what I'm gonna do.
3. You know I'm gonna leave,   you know I'm gonna go.
4. You know I'm gonna leave,   you know I'm gonna go, woman.
5. I'm gonna leave, woman,   goodbye, American Woman.
6. Goodbye, American chick,   goodbye, American broad.

Chorus 2. American Woman, get away from me   3. American Woman, said get away
American Woman, mama let me be   American Woman, listen what I say
Don't come knockin' around my door   Don't come hangin' around my door
Don't wanna see your shadow no more   Don't wanna see your face no more
Colored lights can hypnotize   I don't need your war machines
Sparkle someone else's eyes   I don't need your ghetto scenes
Now woman, I said get away   Colored lights can hypnotize
American Woman, listen what I say.   Sparkle someone else's eyes
                                           Now woman, get away from me
                                           American Woman, mama let me be.

Annie's Song

Words and Music by
John Denver

Bang a Gong
(Get It On)

Words and Music by
Marc Bolan

2. You're built like a car
   You've got a hub cap diamond star halo
   You're built like a car oh yeah
   You're an untamed youth that's the truth
   With your cloak full of eagles
   You're dirty sweet and you're my girl.

3. You're windy and wild
   You've got the blues in your shoes and your stockings
   You're windy and wild oh yeah
   You're built like a car
   You've got a hub cap diamond star halo
   You're dirty sweet and you're my girl.

4. You're dirty and sweet
   Clad in black, don't look back and I love you.
   You're dirty and sweet oh yeah
   You dance when you walk
   So let's dance, take a chance, understand me
   You're dirty sweet and you're my girl.

   To Chorus and Fade

Beach Baby

Words and Music by
John Carter and Gill Shakespeare

I did - n't rec - og - nize the girl next door, ___ the
That's where you told me that you'd wear my ring, ___ the I

beat - up sneak - ers, and the pon - y - tail. ___
guess you don't ___ re - mem - ber an - y - thing. ___

Beach ba - by, beach ba - by

give me your hand, ___ give me some - thing that I ___ can re - mem -

ber, _____ just like be - fore _ we could walk _ by the shore _ in the moon -

light. _____ Beach ba - by, beach ba - by

there on the sand _ from Ju - ly _____ to the end _ of Sep - tem - ber, _____

surf - ing was fun, _ we'd be out ___ in the sun _ ev - 'ry day. _____

To Coda

Ah _____ ah _____

ah _____ ah

Beach ba - by, beach ba - by, beach ba - by, beach ba - by,

beach ba - by, beach ba - by do do do do do do

D.S. al Coda

CODA

Repeat and Fade

The Boss

Words and Music by
Nickolas Ashford and Valerie Simpson

But love   taught

me   who was,   who was, who was the boss.

Repeat and fade

Love   taught   me   who was the boss.

Repeat and fade

A Boy Named Sue

Words and Music by
Shel Silverstein

ever did was be - fore he left, he went and named me Sue.

Verse II

2. Well, he must have thought it was quite a joke, And it

got lots of laughs from - a lots of folks, It seems I had to fight my whole life

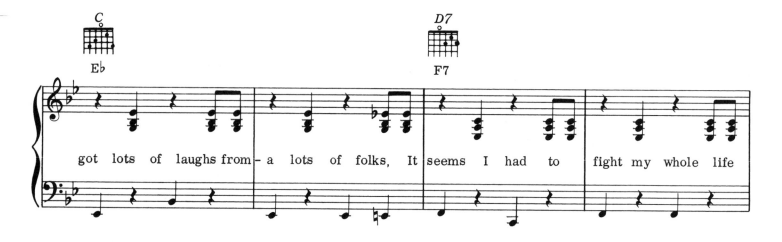

through.

Some gal would giggle and I'd get red, And

some guy would laugh and I'd bust his head; I tell you, life ain't easy for a boy named Sue.

For repeats | *Last time*

3. (Well,) I grew up quick and I grew up mean, My fist got hard and my wits got keen,
Roamed from town to town to hide my shame. But I made me a vow to the moon and stars:
I'd search the honky tonks and bars and kill that man that give me that awful name.

4. But it was Gatlinburg in mid-July and I had just hit town and my throat was dry,
I'd thought I'd stop and have myself a brew. At an old saloon on a street of mud
And at a table dealing stud sat the dirty, mangy dog that named me Sue.

5. Well, I knew that snake was my own sweet dad from a worn-out picture that my mother had,
And I knew that scar on his cheek and his evil eye. He was big and bent and gray and old,
And I looked at him and my blood ran cold, and I said "My name is Sue. How do you do.
Now you're gonna die." Yeah, that's what I told him.

6. Well, I hit him right between the eyes and he went down, but to my surprise he come up with a knife
And cut off a piece of my ear. But I busted a chair right across his teeth, And we crashed through
the wall and into the street, Kicking and a-gouging in the mud and the blood and the beer.

7. I tell you I've fought tougher men but I really can't remember when,
He kicked like a mule and he bit like a crocodile. I heard him laughin' and then I heard him cussin',
He went for his gun and I pulled mine first. He stood there looking at me and I saw him smile.

8. And he said, "Son, this world is rough and if a man's gonna make it, he's gotta be tough;
And I knew I wouldn't be there to help you along. So I give you that name and I said 'Goodbye;'
I knew you'd have to get tough or die. And it's that name that helped to make you strong."

9. "Yeah," he said, "Now you have just fought one helluva fight, and I know you hate me and you've
got the right to kill me now, and I wouldn't blame you if you do. But you ought to thank me
before I die for the gravel in your guts and the spit in your eye because I'm the _ _ _ _
that named you Sue."

Yeah, what could I do? What could I do?

10. I got all choked up and I threw down my gun. Called him a pa and he called me a son,
And I come away with a different point of view. And I think about him now and then.
Every time I tried, every time I win and if I ever have a son I think I am gonna name him
Bill or George — anything but Sue.

Candida

Words and Music by
Toni Wine and Irwin Levine

Diamond Girl

Words and Music by
James Seals and Dash Crofts

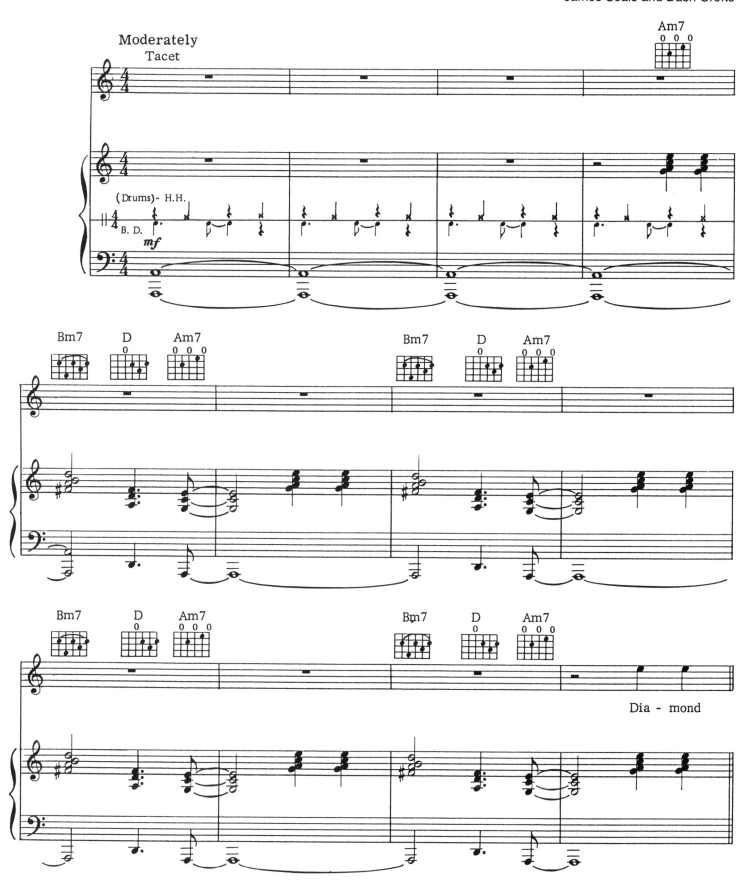

39

such a rare thing, ra-di-ant child.

Shuffle rhythm (♩♩ = ♩³♪)

I could nev-er find _____ an-oth-er one like_

_ you,_____ part of me _____

is deep down in-side_ you.___ Can't you feel_

the whole world's a - turn - in',

we are real _____ and we are a - burn-

in', _____ hey. ____ Dia - mond girl, _____

now that I've found ___ you, _____ well, it's a - round ___

42

you that I am, a - woah

woah, oh, oh.

Dia - mond

44

Three times

Bm7 D Am7 Bm7 D Am7

girl, you sure do__ shine. Dia - mond

Three times

Bm7 D Am7 Gmaj7 Fmaj7 C/E Dm7

girl, you sure do__ shine. _____

Am7

(Guitar ad lib.)

3

(Horns)

Repeat and fade

Am7

Repeat and fade

45

Cold As Ice

Words and Music by
Mick Jones and Lou Gramm

Some-day you'll __ pay the price, I know. I've
seen it be-fore; __ it hap-pens all the time. __ You're clos-ing the door; __ you leave the
world be-hind. __ You're dig-ging for gold __ yet throw-ing a-way __ a
for-tune in feel — ings, but some-day you'll pay.

47

some-day you'll pay.

Cold   as

Disco Inferno

Words and Music by
Leroy Green and Tyrone G. Kersey

Feels Like the First Time

Words and Music by
Mick Jones

Moderate Rock beat

I would climb an-y moun-tain,
I have wait-ed a life-time,

sail a-cross a
spent my time so

storm-y sea,
fool-ish-ly.

if that's what it takes me, ba-by,
But now that I've found you,

Georgy Porgy

Words and Music by
David Paich

It's not __ your sit - u - a - tion. I just __ need con -
Just think __ how long __ I've known __ ya. It's wrong __ for me __

tem - pla - tion o - ver you. __
__ to own __ ya, lock and key. __

I'm not __ so sys - tem - at - ic. It's just __ that I'm __
It's real - ly not __ con - fus - in'. I'm just __ the young __

Give a Little Bit

Words and Music by
Rick Davies and Roger Hodgson

So, give a lit - tle bit, _____

oh, give a lit - tle bit _____ of your time _____ to me.

See the man _____ with the lone - ly eyes? _____ Oh,

take his hand; _____ you'll be _____ sur - prised. _____

Have You Never Been Mellow

Written by John Farrar

Now I don't mean   to make you frown;
Now you're not hard   to un - der - stand;

no, I just want   you to slow down.
you need some - one to take your hand.

cresc.

Have you nev-er been

mf

mel - low?   Have you nev-er tried   to find a com-

Got to Be Real

Words and Music by
David Foster, David Paich
and Cheryl Lynn

Hold the Line

Words and Music by
David Paich

It's not in the way_____ that you hold me.
It's not in the words_____ that you told me.

I Am Woman

Words by Helen Reddy

Music by Ray Burton

ev - er gon - na keep____ me down a - gain.   Oh,____ yes, I am wise____ but it's wis-

- dom born of pain._____   Yes, I paid the price,____   but look how much____ I gained.____ If I

have to____ I can do an - y - thing.____   I am strong,   I am in-

vin - ci - ble,____   I am wom - an.____

To Coda

I Honestly Love You

Words and Music by
Peter Allen and Jeff Barry

I'd Really Love to See You Tonight

Words and Music by
Parker McGee

Knock Three Times

Words and Music by
Irwin Levine and L. Russell Brown

I can feel your bod - y sway - in', _____
in my si - lence I a - dore _____ you, _____ and

one floor be - low me, you don't e - ven know me, I
on - ly in my dreams did that wall be - tween us come a -

D   G

love _____ you. }
part. _____ }   Oh, my dar - lin',   knock three times on the ceil - ing if you

D   A7

want _ me; _   Twice on the pipe

90

I'm Every Woman

Words and Music by
Nickolas Ashford and Valerie Simpson

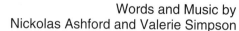

I'm ev - 'ry wom - an. It's all ___ in ___

me. _____ An - y - thing __ you want done, ba - by,

Cm

I'll do it nat - 'ral - ly. _____

Fm9

I'm ev - 'ry wom - an. It's all __ in _____ me. _____

{ 1.2. I can read your thoughts right now. ___ Ev - 'ry word from A __ to Z. }
{ 3. An - y - thing you want done, ba - by, I'll do it nat - 'ral - ly. }

An - y time ___ you feel ___ dan - ger ___ or fear, ___ in - stant -
And when it ___ comes down ___ to some good old - fash - ioned love, ___ that's what

1.

ly I ___ will ap - pear, _____ 'cause

2.

D.S. al Coda

I've got, hon - ey, I've _____ got.

Coda

woh. I ain't brag - gin',

Last Dance

Words and Music by
Paul Jabara

Let's Stay Together

Words and Music by
Al Green, Willie Mitchell
and Al Jackson, Jr.

Moderate rock

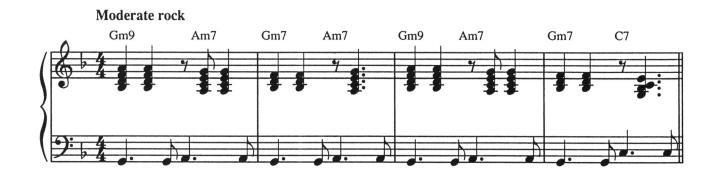

Verse:

1. I'm _____ I'm so in love with you. _____
(2.) since, ba - by, _____ since we've been to - geth - er _____
3. Why, _____ why peo - ple break up _____

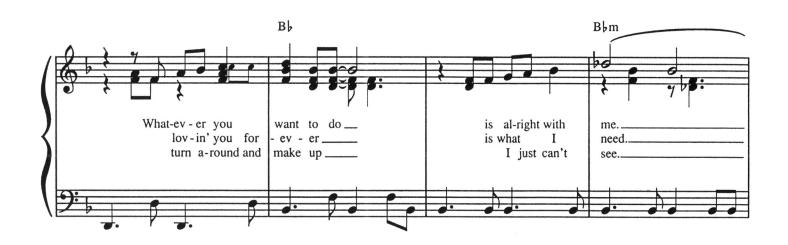

What-ev - er you want to do _____ is al-right with me.
lov-in' you for - ev - er _____ is what I need.
turn a-round and make up _____ I just can't see.

good or bad, _____ hap-py or sad. _____

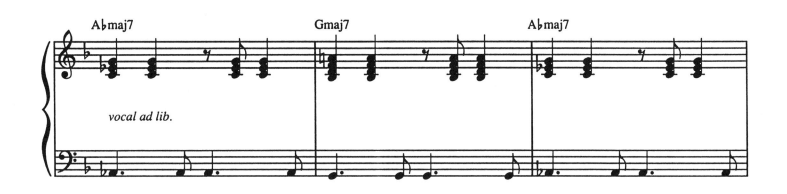

vocal ad lib.

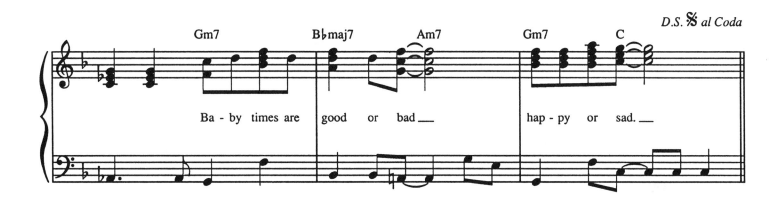

Ba - by times are good or bad _____ hap-py or sad. _____

D.S. 𝄋 al Coda

Babe _____ let's stay to - geth - er. _____

Repeat ad lib. and fade

103

Lido Shuffle

Words and Music by
Boz Scaggs and David Paich

In a tomb-stone bar ___ in a juke-
Li - do be run - nin' hav - in'

joint car ___ he made ___ a stop ___
great big fun un - til he got ___ the note ___

just long ___ e - nough ___ to grab ___
say - ing, "Tow ___ the line ___ or blow

___ the han - dle off ___ the top. ___
it," and that ___ was all ___ she wrote. ___

Next ____ stop Chi - town, Li -
He be mak - in' like a bee - line

do put the mon - ey down and let ____ it roll. ___
head - in' for the bor - der line, go - in' for broke ___

He said, "One more __ job ____ ought to get it,
say - in', "One more __ hit ____ ought to do it,

one last __ shot ____ 'fore we quit it,
this joint __ ain't ____ noth - in' to it,

one one for the road." _____
one more for the road." _____

Li - do, oh, _____

he's for the mon - ey, he's _

_ for the show, _ Li - do's a - wait - in' for _____ the go.

A Little More Love

Written by John Farrar

'til you have to go home. ___
in the warmth of your arms, ___

No's a word I can't say. ___
in the web of your lies. ___

'Cause it gets me no - where ___

to tell you no, ___

and it gets me no - where ___

to make you go. ___

Will a lit-tle more love make you

Looks Like We Made It

Words and Music by
Richard Kerr and Will Jennings

strong, when old feel - ings start to stir. ___ Looks like we
minds, could I ev - er let you go? ___ Oh no, we've

made it. }
made it. }
Left each oth - er on ___ the way to an - oth - er love, ___

Looks like we made it, or I

thought so till to - day ___ un - til you were there ev - 'ry - where. And

Lowdown

Words and Music by
Boz Scaggs and David Paich

Magic

Written by John Farrar

1. Come take___ my hand,___ you should know___ me,___ I've
2. Build-ing___ your dream___ has to start___ now,___ there's

3. 4. (see additional lyrics)

al-ways been in___your___ mind.___ You know I will be
no oth-er road_ to ___ take.___ You won't make a mis-

kind, I'll be guid - ing_____ you. - ing_____ you._____
take, I'll be guid -

Chorus:

You have to be - lieve_____ we are

mag - ic,_____ noth - ing can stand__ in our way._____ You

have to be - lieve__ we are ma - gic,_____ don't let your aim__ ev - er stray._____

Verse 3:
From where I stand, you are home free;
The planets align so rare, there's promise in the air,
And I'm guiding you.

Verse 4:
Through every turn, I'll be near you,
I'll come anytime you call, I'll catch you when you fall,
I'll be guiding you. (To Chorus:)

Minute by Minute

Words by
Michael McDonald and Lester Abrams

Music by Michael McDonald

you should spend your life with some - one,

you could spend your life with some - one.

Repeat and fade

Min-ute by min-ute by min-ute by min-ute, I'll be hold - in'

on. ____

126

Misty Blue

Words and Music by
Bob Montgomery

Slowly

C   C+   F6   G7

Oh, it's been such a long, long, time, Looks like I'd get you

C   C7   F   Dm   G6   G7

off my mind. Oh, but I can't; just the thought of you Turns my whole world a

C   C+   F6   G7

mist - y blue. Just a men -tion of your name Turns the flick - er

99

Words and Music by
David Paich

Say, Has Anybody Seen My Sweet Gypsy Rose

Words and Music by
Larry Russell Brown and Irwin Levine

*Recorded a half step lower.

135

On and On

Words and Music by
Stephen Bishop

Rocky Mountain High

Words and Music by
John Denver and Mike Taylor

*Guitarists: Tune low E down to D.

Sentimental Lady

Words and Music by
Robert Welch

You are here and warm __ but

I could look a-way ___ and you'd __ be gone. ___ 'Cause

we live in a time _ when mean-ing falls in splin-ters from our lives. That's

why I've trav-eled far, 'cause I come so to - geth-er where you are. ___ Yes, and

all of the things that I said that I want-ed come rush-ing by in my head when I'm with you.

Four - teen joys and a will to be mer - ry. All of the things that they say are ver - y

sen - ti - men - tal gen - tle wind ___ blow - ing through ___ my life a - gain. ___

So Very Hard to Go

Words and Music by
Stephen Kupka and Emilio Castillo

Ain't noth-in' I can say,_____ noth-in' I can
I knew the time would come_____ I'd have to pay for my mis-

do._____
takes._____

I feel so bad,
I can't blame you for what you're do-in' to me,

make_____ you un-hap-py.

No, I could-n't do that,

girl.___ On-ly wish I did-n't love you so;

makes it so ver-y hard to

go._____ 'Cause I love you so.___

(So ver-y hard to go.)

To Coda

(So ver-y hard to go.)

1.

I love you so.___

Summer Breeze

Words and Music by
James Seals and Dash Crofts

See the cur - tains hang - in' in the win - dow___ in the eve - ning on a Fri - day night.___
See the pa - per lay - in' on the side - walk, _ a lit - tle mu - sic from the house next door.___

mind. _____ Sum-mer breeze __

makes me feel fine, __ blow-in' through the jas - mine in my mind. _____

See the smile a wait - in' in the kitch - en, food cook-in' and the plates for two._____

_____   Feel the arms that reach_ out to hold_ me _

in the eve-ning when the day is through._____

Take Me Home, Country Roads

Words and Music by
John Denver, Bill Danoff
and Taffy Nivert

young - er than the moun - tains___ grow - in' like a breeze.___

mist - y taste of moon - shine,___ tear - drop in my eye.___

Coun -try Roads,_____ take me home _____ to the

place _____ I be - long:_____ West Vir - gin - ia,___

moun-tain mom -ma,_____ Take me home,_____ Coun-try

Roads._____ All my

I hear her voice, in the

166

Superstar

Words and Music by
Leon Russell and Bonnie Sheridan

Swearin' to God

Words and Music by
Denny Randell and Bob Crewe

Moderately, with a steady beat

Swear-in' to God, __

there's no one else on earth I'd

170

171

175

This Masquerade

Words and Music by
Leon Russell

179

*Guitar solo sounds 8va
  lower than written.

Tie a Yellow Ribbon
Round the Ole Oak Tree

Words and Music by
L. Russell Brown and Irwin Levine

1. I'm com-in' home,___ I've done my time,___ now I've
2. Bus driv-er please___ look for me,___ 'cause I

got to know___ what is___ and is-n't mine.___ If
could-n't bear___ to see___ what I might see.___ I'm

you re-ceived my let-ter tell-in' you___ I'd soon be free,___
real-ly still in pris-on and my love___ she holds the key,___

a

then you'll know just what to do___ if you still want me,
sim-ple yel-low rib-bon's what I if need to set want me free, me,

I

if you still want me.
wrote and told her me. please.

Chorus:

Tie a yel-low rib-bon round the ole oak tree,___ it's been

183

You Are So Beautiful

Words and Music by
Billy Preston and Bruce Fisher

Cherry Lane Music is your source for JOHN DENVER SONGBOOKS!

PIANO/VOCAL BOOKS

JOHN DENVER ANTHOLOGY
A collection of 54 of this music legend's greatest tunes, including: Annie's Song • Follow Me • Leaving on a Jet Plane • Rocky Mountain High • Sunshine on My Shoulders • and more, plus a biography and John's reflections on his many memorable songs.
_____02502165 Piano/Vocal/Guitar $22.95

THE BEST OF JOHN DENVER – EASY PIANO
A collection of 18 Denver classics arranged for easy piano. Contains: Leaving on a Jet Plane • Take Me Home, Country Roads • Rocky Mountain High • Follow Me • and more.
_____02505512 Easy Piano $9.95

THE BEST OF JOHN DENVER – PIANO SOLOS
Best of John Denver – Piano Solos is a fabulous collection of 10 greatest hits from the legendary country artist. It includes many of his major hits including: Annie's Song • Leaving on a Jet Plane • Rocky Mountain High • and Take Me Home, Country Roads.
_____02503629 Piano Solo $10.95

JOHN DENVER – A CELEBRATION OF LIFE
The matching folio to the legendary songwriter/performer's album features some of his most popular songs. Includes: Rocky Mountain High • Leaving on a Jet Plane • Whispering Jesse • and more, plus photos and biographical information.
_____02502227 Piano/Vocal/Guitar...$14.95

A JOHN DENVER CHRISTMAS
A delightful collection of Christmas songs and carols recorded by John Denver. Includes traditional carols (Deck the Halls • Hark! The Herald Angels Sing • The Twelve Days of Christmas) as well as such contemporary songs as: A Baby Just Like You • Christmas for Cowboys • Christmas Like a Lullaby • and The Peace Carol.
_____02500002 Piano/Vocal/Guitar...$14.95

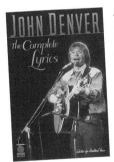

JOHN DENVER: THE COMPLETE LYRICS
An extremely gifted singer/songwriter, John Denver possessed the unique ability to marry melodic music with gentle, thought-provoking words that endeared him to his countless fans. Now, for the first time ever, John Denver's lyrics have been printed in their entirety: no other book like this exists! It contains lyrics to more than 200 songs, and includes an annotated discography showing all the songs, and an index of first lines. This collection also features an introduction by Tom Paxton, and a foreword from Milt Okun, John Denver's first record producer, and the founder of Cherry Lane Music.
_____02500459 ....$16.95

JOHN DENVER'S GREATEST HITS
This collection combines all of the songs from Denver's three best-selling greatest hits albums. 34 songs in all, including: Leaving on a Jet Plane • For Baby (For Bobbie) • Thank God I'm a Country Boy • Annie's Song • Perhaps Love • I Want to Live.
_____02502166 Piano/Vocal/Guitar $17.95

JOHN DENVER – A LEGACY OF SONG
This collection celebrates one of the world's most popular and prolific entertainers. Features 25 of John's best-loved songs with his commentary on each: Annie's Song • Fly Away • Leaving on a Jet Plane • Rocky Mountain High • Sunshine on My Shoulders • Take Me Home, Country Roads • Thank God I'm a Country Boy • and more, plus a biography, discography, reflections on John's numerous accomplishments, and photos spanning his entire career.
_____02502151 Piano/Vocal/Guitar Softcover $24.95
_____02502152 Piano/Vocal/Guitar Hardcover $34.95

JOHN DENVER & THE MUPPETS – A CHRISTMAS TOGETHER
Back by popular demand! This book featuring John Denver, Kermit, and all the Muppets includes 12 holiday songs: A Baby Just like You • Carol for a Christmas Tree • Christmas Is Coming • The Christmas Wish • Deck the Halls • Have Yourself a Merry Little Christmas • Little Saint Nick • Noel: Christmas Eve, 1913 • The Peace Carol • Silent Night, Holy Night • The Twelve Days of Christmas • We Wish You a Merry Christmas.
_____02500501 Piano/Vocal/Guitar...$9.95

JOHN DENVER – THE WILDLIFE CONCERT
This matching folio to John Denver's second live album – a two-CD set accompanying a cable TV special and home video – features 29 fabulous tracks: Amazon • Annie's Song • Bet on the Blues • Calypso • Darcy Farrow • Eagles and Horses • Falling Out of Love • The Harder They Fall • Is It Love? • Leaving on a Jet Plane • Me and My Uncle • A Song for All Lovers • Sunshine on My Shoulders • You Say That the Battle Is Over • and more.
_____02500326 Piano/Vocal/Guitar...........................$17.95

P/V/G SHEET MUSIC

_____02504223 Annie's Song..$3.95
_____02504206 Follow Me...$3.95
_____02504181 For You $3.95
_____02504225 Leaving on a Jet Plane....................................$3.95
_____02509538 Perhaps Love $3.95
_____02504219 Sunshine on My Shoulders.............................$3.95
_____02504214 Take Me Home, Country Roads $3.95
_____02509523 Thank God I'm a Country Boy.........................$3.95

GUITAR BOOKS

JOHN DENVER ANTHOLOGY FOR EASY GUITAR
This superb collection of 42 great Denver songs made easy for guitar includes: Annie's Song • Leaving on a Jet Plane • Take Me Home, Country Roads • plus performance notes, a biography, and Denver's thoughts on the songs.
_____02506878 Easy Guitar..$15.95

JOHN DENVER AUTHENTIC GUITAR STYLE
12 never-before-published acoustic guitar note-for-note transcriptions of the most popular songs by John Denver. Includes the hits: Annie's Song • Sunshine on My Shoulders • Take Me Home, Country Roads • and more.
_____02506901 Acoustic Guitar Transcriptions $14.95

THE BEST OF JOHN DENVER
Over 20 of Denver's best-known hits spanning his 25-year career! Includes: Annie's Song • Leaving on a Jet Plane • Rocky Mountain High • Thank God I'm a Country Boy • Sunshine on My Shoulders • and more.
_____02506879 Easy Guitar $9.95

JOHN DENVER – GREATEST HITS FOR FINGERSTYLE GUITAR
For the first time ever, 11 favorite Denver standards in fingerstyle arrangements that incorporate the melodies of the songs and can therefore be played as solo guitar pieces or vocal accompaniments. Includes: Annie's Song • Leaving on a Jet Plane • Rocky Mountain High • and more.
_____02506928 Fingerstyle Guitar..$14.95

For a complete listing of available Cherry Lane titles, please visit our web site at **www.cherrylane.com**

CHERRY LANE MUSIC COMPANY
6 East 32nd Street, New York, NY 10016
Quality in Printed Music

EXCLUSIVELY DISTRIBUTED BY
HAL•LEONARD CORPORATION
7777 W. BLUEMOUND RD. P.O. BOX 13819 MILWAUKEE, WI 53213

More Big-Note & Easy Piano Books

For a complete listing of Cherry Lane titles available, including contents listings, please visit our web site at www.cherrylane.com

CLASSICAL CHRISTMAS
Easy solo arrangements of 30 wonderful holiday songs: Ave Maria • Dance of the Sugar Plum Fairy • Evening Prayer • Gesu Bambino • Hallelujah! • He Shall Feed His Flock • March of the Toys • O Come, All Ye Faithful • O Holy Night • Pastoral Symphony • Sheep May Safely Graze • Sinfonia • Waltz of the Flowers • and more.
___02500112 Easy Piano Solo $9.95

BEST OF JOHN DENVER
___02505512 Easy Piano $9.95

DOWN THE AISLE
Easy piano arrangements of 20 beloved pop and classical wedding songs, including: Air on the G String • Ave Maria • Canon in D • Follow Me • Give Me Forever (I Do) • Jesu, Joy of Man's Desiring • Prince of Denmark's March • Through the Years • Trumpet Tune • Unchained Melody • Wedding March • When I Fall in Love • You Decorated My Life • and more.
___025000267 Easy Piano $9.95

EASY BROADWAY SHOWSTOPPERS
Easy piano arrangements of 16 traditional and new Broadway standards, including: "Impossible Dream" from *Man of La Mancha* • "Unusual Way" from *Nine* • "This Is the Moment" from *Jekyll & Hyde* • many more.
___02505517 Easy Piano $12.95

GOLD AND GLORY – THE ROAD TO EL DORADO
This beautiful souvenir songbook features full-color photos and 8 songs from the DreamWorks animated film. Includes original songs by Elton John and Tim Rice, and a score by Hans Zimmer and John Powell. Songs: Cheldorado – Score • El Dorado • Friends Never Say Goodbye • It's Tough to Be a God • Someday out of the Blue (Theme from El Dorado) • The Trail We Blaze • Without Question • Wonders of the New World: To Shibalba.
___02500274 Easy Piano $14.95

A FAMILY CHRISTMAS AROUND THE PIANO
25 songs for hours of family fun, including: Away in a Manger • Deck the Hall • The First Noel • God Rest Ye Merry, Gentlemen • Hark! the Herald Angels Sing • Jingle Bells • Jolly Old St. Nicholas • Joy to the World • O Little Town of Bethlehem • Silent Night, Holy Night • The Twelve Days of Christmas • and more.
___02500398 Easy Piano $7.95

GILBERT & SULLIVAN FOR EASY PIANO
20 great songs from 6 great shows by this beloved duo renowned for their comedic classics. Includes: Behold the Lord High Executioner • The Flowers That Bloom in the Spring • He Is an Englishman • I Am the Captain of the Pinafore • (I'm Called) Little Buttercup • Miya Sama • Three Little Maids • Tit-Willow • We Sail the Ocean Blue • When a Merry Maiden Marries • When Britain Really Ruled the Waves • When Frederic Was a Lad • and more.
___02500270 Easy Piano $12.95

GREAT CONTEMPORARY BALLADS
___02500150 Easy Piano $12.95

HOLY CHRISTMAS CAROLS COLORING BOOK
A terrific songbook with 7 sacred carols and lots of coloring pages for the young pianist. Songs include: Angels We Have Heard on High • The First Noel • Hark! The Herald Angels Sing • It Came upon a Midnight Clear • O Come All Ye Faithful • O Little Town of Bethlehem • Silent Night.
___02500277 Five-Finger Piano $6.95

JEKYLL & HYDE – VOCAL SELECTIONS
Ten songs from the Wildhorn/Bricusse Broadway smash, arranged for big-note: In His Eyes • It's a Dangerous Game • Lost in the Darkness • A New Life • No One Knows Who I Am • Once Upon a Dream • Someone Like You • Sympathy, Tenderness • Take Me as I Am • This Is the Moment.
___02505515 Easy Piano $12.95
___02500023 Big-Note Piano $9.95

JUST FOR KIDS – *NOT!* CHRISTMAS SONGS
This unique collection of 14 Christmas favorites is fun for the whole family! Kids can play the full-sounding big-note solos alone, or with their parents (or teachers) playing accompaniment for the thrill of four-hand piano! Includes: Deck the Halls • Jingle Bells • Silent Night • What Child Is This? • and more.
___02505510 Big-Note Piano $7.95

JUST FOR KIDS – *NOT!* CLASSICS
Features big-note arrangements of classical masterpieces, plus optional accompaniment for adults. Songs: Air on the G String • Dance of the Sugar Plum Fairy • Für Elise • Jesu, Joy of Man's Desiring • Ode to Joy • Pomp and Circumstance • The Sorcerer's Apprentice • William Tell Overture • and more!
___02505513 Classics....................$7.95
___02500301 More Classics $7.95

JUST FOR KIDS – *NOT!* FUN SONGS
Fun favorites for kids everywhere in big-note arrangements for piano, including: Bingo • Eensy Weensy Spider • Farmer in the Dell • Jingle Bells • London Bridge • Pop Goes the Weasel • Puff the Magic Dragon • Skip to My Lou • Twinkle, Twinkle Little Star • and more!
___02505523 Fun Songs................$7.95
___02505528 More Fun Songs $7.95

JUST FOR KIDS – *NOT!* TV THEMES & MOVIE SONGS
Entice the kids to the piano with this delightful collection of songs and themes from movies and TV. These big-note arrangements include themes from The Brady Bunch and The Addams Family, as well as Do-Re-Mi (The Sound of Music), theme from Beetlejuice (Day-O) and Puff the Magic Dragon. Each song includes an accompaniment part for teacher or adult so that the kids can experience the joy of four-hand playing as well! Plus performance tips.
___02505507 TV Themes & Movie Songs $9.95
___02500304 More TV Themes & Movie Songs $9.95

LOVE BALLADS
___02500152 EZ-Play Today #364 $7.95

MERRY CHRISTMAS, EVERYONE
Over 20 contemporary and classic all-time holiday favorites arranged for big-note piano or easy piano. Includes: Away in a Manger • Christmas Like a Lullaby • The First Noel • Joy to the World • The Marvelous Toy • and more.
___02505600 Big-Note Piano $9.95

See your local music dealer or contact:

CHERRY LANE MUSIC COMPANY
6 East 32nd Street, New York, NY 10016

EXCLUSIVELY DISTRIBUTED BY

HAL•LEONARD®
7777 W. BLUEMOUND RD. P.O. BOX 13819 MILWAUKEE, WI 53213

POKEMON 2 B.A. MASTER
This great songbook features easy piano arrangements of 13 tunes from the hit TV series: 2.B.A. Master • Double Trouble (Team Rocket) • Everything Changes • Misty's Song • My Best Friends • Pokémon (Dance Mix) • Pokémon Theme • PokéRAP • The Time Has Come (Pikachu's Goodbye) • Together, Forever • Viridian City • What Kind of Pokémon Are You? • You Can Do It (If You Really Try). Includes a full-color, 8-page pull-out section featuring characters and scenes from this super hot show.
___02500145 Easy Piano $12.95

POKEMON
Five-finger arrangements of 7 songs from the hottest show for kids! Includes: Pokémon Theme • The Time Has Come (Pikachu's Goodbye) • 2B A Master • Together, Forever • What Kind of Pokémon Are You? • You Can Do It (If You Really Try). Also features cool character artwork, and a special section listing the complete lyrics for the "PokéRAP."
___02500291 Five-Finger Piano $7.95

POP/ROCK HITS
___02500153 E-Z Play Today #366 $7.95

POP/ROCK LOVE SONGS
Easy arrangements of 18 romatic favorites, including: Always • Bed of Roses • Butterfly Kisses • Follow Me • From This Moment On • Hard Habit to Break • Leaving on a Jet Plane • When You Say Nothing at All • more.
___02500151 Easy Piano $10.95

POPULAR CHRISTMAS CAROLS COLORING BOOK
Kids are sure to love this fun holiday songbook! It features five-finger piano arrangements of seven Christmas classics, complete with coloring pages throughout. Songs include: Deck the Hall • Good King Wenceslas • Jingle Bells • Jolly Old St. Nicholas • O Christmas Tree • Up on the Housetop • We Wish You a Merry Christmas.
___02500276 Five-Finger Piano $6.95

PUFF THE MAGIC DRAGON & 54 OTHER ALL-TIME CHILDREN'S FAVORITE SONGS
55 timeless songs enjoyed by generations of kids, and sure to be favorites for years to come. Songs include: A-Tisket A-Tasket • Alouette • Eensy Weensy Spider • The Farmer in the Dell • I've Been Working on the Railroad • If You're Happy and You Know It • Joy to the World • Michael Finnegan • Oh Where, Oh Where Has My Little Dog Gone • Silent Night • Skip to My Lou • This Old Man • and many more.
___02500017 Big-Note Piano $12.95

PURE ROMANCE
___02500268 Easy Piano $10.95

SCHOOLHOUSE ROCK SONGBOOK
10 unforgettable songs from the classic television educational series, now experiencing a booming resurgence in popularity from Generation X'ers to today's kids! Includes: I'm Just a Bill • Conjunction Junction • Lolly, Lolly, Lolly (Get Your Adverbs Here) • The Great American Melting Pot • and more.
___02505576 Big-Note Piano $8.95

BEST OF JOHN TESH
___02505511 Easy Piano $12.95
___02500128 E-Z Play Today #356 $8.95

TOP COUNTRY HITS
___02500154 E-Z Play Today #365 $7.95

great songs series

Cherry Lane Music is proud to present this legendary series which has delighted players and performers for generations.

Great Songs of the Fifties

The latest release in Cherry Lane's acclaimed Great Songs series, this songbook presents 51 musical memories from the fabulous '50s! Features rock, pop, country, Broadway and movie tunes, including: All Shook Up • At the Hop • Blue Suede Shoes • Dream Lover • Fly Me to the Moon • Kansas City • Love Me Tender • Misty • Peggy Sue • Rock Around the Clock • Sea of Love • Sixteen Tons • Take the "A" Train • Wonderful! Wonderful! • and more. Includes an introduction by award-winning journalist Bruce Pollock.
_____02500323 P/V/G..............................$16.95

Great Songs of the Sixties, Vol. 1 – Revised Edition

The newly updated version of this classic book includes 80 faves from the 1960s: Angel of the Morning • Bridge over Troubled Water • Cabaret • Different Drum • Do You Believe in Magic • Eve of Destruction • Georgy Girl • It Was a Very Good Year • Monday, Monday • People • Spinning Wheel • Walk on By • and more.
_____02509902 P/V/G............................$19.95

Great Songs of the Sixties, Vol. 2 – Revised Edition

61 more 60s hits: And When I Die • California Dreamin' • Crying • The 59th Street Bridge Song (Feelin' Groovy) • For Once in My Life • Honey • Little Green Apples • MacArthur Park • Me and Bobby McGee • Nowhere Man • Piece of My Heart • Sugar, Sugar • You Made Me So Very Happy • and more.
_____02509904 P/V/G............................$19.95

Great Songs of the Seventies – Revised Edition

This super collection of 70 big hits from the '70s includes: After the Love Has Gone • Afternoon Delight • Annie's Song • Band on the Run • Cold as Ice • FM • Imagine • It's Too Late • Layla • Let It Be • Maggie May • Piano Man • Shelter from the Storm • Superstar • Sweet Baby James • Time in a Bottle • The Way We Were • more!
_____02509917 P/V/G............................$19.95

Prices, contents, and availability subject to change without notice.

Great Songs of the Seventies – Volume 2

Features 58 outstanding '70s songs in rock, pop, country, Broadway and movie genres: American Woman • Baby, I'm-A Want You • Day by Day • Do That to Me One More Time • Dog & Butterfly • Don't Cry Out Loud • Dreamboat Annie • Follow Me • Get Closer • Grease • Heard It in a Love Song • I'll Be There • It's a Heartache • The Loco-Motion • My Eyes Adored You • New Kid in Town • Night Fever • On and On • Sing • Summer Breeze • Tonight's the Night • We Are the Champions • Y.M.C.A. • and more. Includes articles by Cherry Lane Music Company founder Milt Okun, and award-winning music journalist Bruce Pollock.
_____02500322 P/V/G............................$19.95

Great Songs of the Eighties – Revised Edition

This newly revised edition features 50 songs in rock, pop & country styles, plus hits from Broadway and the movies! Songs: Almost Paradise • Angel of the Morning • Do You Really Want to Hurt Me • Endless Love • Flashdance...What a Feeling • Guilty • Hungry Eyes • (Just Like) Starting Over • Let Love Rule • Missing You • Patience • Through the Years • Time After Time • Total Eclipse of the Heart • and more.
_____02502125 P/V/G............................$18.95

Great Songs of the Nineties

This terrific collection features 48 big hits in many styles. Includes: Achy Breaky Heart • Beautiful in My Eyes • Believe • Black Hole Sun • Black Velvet • Blaze of Glory • Building a Mystery • Crash into Me • Fields of Gold • From a Distance • Glycerine • Here and Now • Hold My Hand • I'll Make Love to You • Ironic • Linger • My Heart Will Go On • Waterfalls • Wonderwall • and more.
_____02500040 P/V/G............................$16.95

Great Songs of the Pop Era

Over 50 hits from the pop era, including: Amazed • Annie's Song • Ebony and Ivory • Every Breath You Take • Hey Nineteen • I Want to Know What Love Is • I'm Every Woman • Just the Two of Us • Leaving on a Jet Plane • My Cherie Amour • Raindrops Keep Fallin' on My Head • Rocky Mountain High • This Is the Moment • Time After Time • (I've Had) the Time of My Life • What a Wonderful World • and more!
_____02500043 Easy Piano $16.95

CHERRY LANE MUSIC COMPANY
6 East 32nd Street, New York, NY 10016
Quality in Printed Music
Visit Cherry Lane on the Internet at
www.cherrylane.com

EXCLUSIVELY DISTRIBUTED BY

HAL•LEONARD CORPORATION
7777 W. BLUEMOUND RD. P.O. BOX 13819 MILWAUKEE, WI 53213

0402

More Great Piano/Vocal Books
Cherry Lane

...ting of Cherry Lane titles available,
...listings, please visit our web site at
www.cherrylane.com